Francis Frith's
AROUND NOTTINGHAM

◆

PHOTOGRAPHIC MEMORIES

Francis Frith's
AROUND NOTTINGHAM

◆

Douglas Whitworth

FRITH
BOOK Co

First published in the United Kingdom in 1999 by
Frith Book Company Ltd

British Library Cataloguing in Publication Data

Around Nottingham
Douglas Whitworth
ISBN 1-85937-060-8

Frith Book Company Ltd
Frith's Barn, Teffont,
Salisbury, Wiltshire SP3 5QP
Tel: +44 (0) 1722 716 376
Email: frithbook.co.uk

Printed and bound in Great Britain

CONTENTS

FRANCIS FRITH: *Victorian Pioneer*

FRANCIS FRITH, Victorian founder of the world-famous photographic archive, was a complex and multitudinous man. A devout Quaker and a highly successful Victorian businessman, he was both philosophic by nature and pioneering in outlook.

By 1855 Francis Frith had already established a wholesale grocery business in Liverpool, and sold it for the astonishing sum of £200,000, which is the equivalent today of over £15,000,000. Now a multi-millionaire, he was able to indulge his passion for travel. As a child he had pored over travel books written by early explorers, and his fancy and imagination had been stirred by family holidays to the sublime mountain regions of Wales and Scotland. 'What a land of spirit-stirring and enriching scenes and places!' he had written. He was to return to these scenes of grandeur in later years to 'recapture the thousands of vivid and tender memories', but with a different purpose. Now in his thirties, and captivated by the new science of photography, Frith set out on a series of pioneering journeys to the Nile regions that occupied him from 1856 until 1860.

INTRIGUE AND ADVENTURE

He took with him on his travels a specially-designed wicker carriage that acted as both dark-room and sleeping chamber. These far-flung journeys were packed with intrigue and adventure. In his life story, written when he was sixty-three, Frith tells of being held captive by bandits, and of fighting 'an awful midnight battle to the very point of surrender with a deadly pack of hungry, wild dogs'. Sporting flowing Arab costume, Frith arrived at Akaba by camel seventy years before Lawrence, where he encountered 'desert princes and rival sheikhs, blazing with jewel-hilted swords'.

During these extraordinary adventures he was assiduously exploring the desert regions bordering the Nile and patiently recording the antiquities and peoples with his camera. He was the first photographer to venture beyond the sixth cataract. Africa was still the mysterious 'Dark Continent', and Stanley and Livingstone's historic meeting was a decade into the future. The conditions for picture taking confound belief. He laboured for hours in his wicker dark-room in the sweltering heat of the desert, while the volatile chemicals fizzed dangerously in their trays. Often he was forced to work in remote tombs and caves

where conditions were cooler. Back in London he exhibited his photographs and was 'rapturously cheered' by members of the Royal Society. His reputation as a photographer was made overnight. An eminent modern historian has likened their impact on the population of the time to that on our own generation of the first photographs taken on the surface of the moon.

VENTURE OF A LIFE-TIME

Characteristically, Frith quickly spotted the opportunity to create a new business as a specialist publisher of photographs. He lived in an era of immense and sometimes violent change. For the poor in the early part of Victoria's reign, work was a drudge and the hours long, and people had precious little free time to enjoy

themselves. Most had no transport other than a cart or gig at their disposal, and had not travelled far beyond the boundaries of their own town or village. However, by the 1870s, the railways had threaded their way across the country, and Bank Holidays and half-day Saturdays had been made obligatory by Act of Parliament. All of a sudden the ordinary working man and his family were able to enjoy days out and see a little more of the world.

With characteristic business acumen, Francis Frith foresaw that these new tourists would enjoy having souvenirs to commemorate their days out. In 1860 he married Mary Ann Rosling and set out with the intention of photographing every city, town and village in Britain. For the next thirty years he travelled the country by train and by pony and trap, producing fine photographs of seaside resorts and beauty spots that were keenly bought by millions of Victorians. These prints were painstakingly pasted into family albums and pored over during the dark nights of winter, rekindling precious memories of summer excursions.

THE RISE OF FRITH & CO

Frith's studio was soon supplying retail shops all over the country. To meet the demand he gathered about him a small team of photographers, and published the work of independent artist-photographers of the calibre of Roger Fenton and Francis Bedford. In order to gain some understanding of the scale of Frith's business one only has to look at the catalogue issued by Frith & Co in 1886: it

runs to some 670 pages, listing not only many thousands of views of the British Isles but also many photographs of most European countries, and China, Japan, the USA and Canada – note the sample page shown above from the hand-written *Frith & Co* ledgers detailing pictures taken. By 1890 Frith had created the greatest specialist photographic publishing company in the world, with over 2,000 outlets – more than the combined number that Boots and W H Smith have today! The picture on the right shows the *Frith & Co* display board at Ingleton in the Yorkshire Dales. Beautifully constructed with mahogany frame and gilt inserts, it could display up to a dozen local scenes.

POSTCARD BONANZA

The ever-popular holiday postcard we know today took many years to develop. In 1870 the Post Office issued the first plain cards, with a pre-printed stamp on one face. In 1894 they allowed other publishers' cards to be sent through the mail with an attached adhesive halfpenny stamp. Demand grew rapidly, and in 1895 a new size of postcard was permitted called the court card, but there was little room for illustration. In 1899, a year after Frith's death, a new card measuring 5½ x 3½ inches became the standard format, but it was not until 1902 that the divided back came into being, with address and message on one face and a full-size illustration on the other. *Frith & Co* were in the vanguard of postcard development, and Frith's sons Eustace and Cyril continued their father's monumental task, expanding the number of views offered to the public and recording more and more places in Britain, as the coasts and countryside were opened up to mass travel.

Francis Frith died in 1898 at his villa in Cannes, his great project still growing. The archive he created continued in business for another seventy years. By 1970 it contained over a third of a million pictures of 7,000 cities, towns and villages. The massive photographic record Frith has left to us stands as a living monument to a special and very remarkable man.

Frith's Archive: *A Unique Legacy*

FRANCIS FRITH'S legacy to us today is of immense significance and value, for the magnificent archive of evocative photographs he created provides a unique record of change in 7,000 cities, towns and villages throughout Britain over a century and more. Frith and his fellow studio photographers revisited locations many times down the years to update their views, compiling for us an enthralling and pageant of British life and character.

We tend to think of Frith's sepia views of Britain as nostalgic, for most of us use them to conjure up memories of places in our own lives with which we have family associations. It often makes us forget that to Francis Frith they were records of daily life as it was actually being lived in the cities, towns and villages of his day. The Victorian age was one of great and often bewildering change for ordinary people, and though the pictures evoke an impression of slower times, life was as busy and hectic as it is today.

We are fortunate that Frith was a photographer of the people, dedicated to recording the minutiae of everyday life. For it is this sheer wealth of visual data, the painstaking chronicle of changes in dress, transport, street layouts, buildings, housing and landscape that captivates us so much today. His remarkable images offer us a powerful link with the past and with the lives of our ancestors.

TODAY'S TECHNOLOGY

Computers have now made it possible for Frith's many thousands of images to be accessed almost instantly. In the Frith archive today, each photograph is carefully 'digitised' then stored on a CD Rom. Frith archivists can locate a single photograph amongst thousands within seconds. Views can be catalogued and sorted under a variety of categories of place and content to the immediate benefit of researchers. Inexpensive reference prints can be created for them at the touch of a mouse button, and a wide range of books and other printed materials assembled and published for a wider, more general readership - in the next twelve months over a hundred Frith local history titles will be

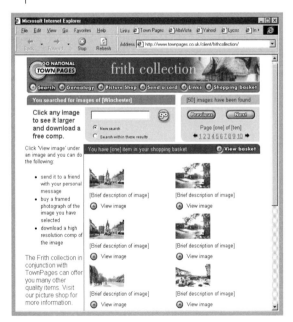

See Frith at www. francisfrith.co.uk

published! The day-to-day workings of the archive are very different from how they were in Francis Frith's time: imagine the herculean task of sorting through eleven tons of glass negatives as Frith had to do to locate a particular sequence of pictures! Yet the archive still prides itself on maintaining the same high standards of excellence laid down by Frith, including the painstaking cataloguing and indexing of every view.

It is curious to reflect on how the internet now allows researchers in America and elsewhere greater instant access to the archive than Frith himself ever enjoyed. Many thousands of individual views can be called up on screen within seconds on one of the Frith internet sites, enabling people living continents away to revisit the streets of their ancestral home town, or view places in Britain where they have enjoyed holidays. Many overseas researchers welcome the chance to view special theme selections, such as transport, sports, costume and ancient monuments.

We are certain that Francis Frith would have heartily approved of these modern developments, for he himself was always working at the very limits of Victorian photographic technology.

THE VALUE OF THE ARCHIVE TODAY

Because of the benefits brought by the computer, Frith's images are increasingly studied by social historians, by researchers into genealogy and ancestry, by architects, town planners, and by teachers and schoolchildren involved in local history projects. In addition, the archive offers every one of us a unique opportunity to examine the places where we and our families have lived and worked down the years. Immensely successful in Frith's own era, the archive is now, a century and more on, entering a new phase of popularity.

THE PAST IN TUNE WITH THE FUTURE

Historians consider the Francis Frith Collection to be of prime national importance. It is the only archive of its kind remaining in private ownership and has been valued at a million pounds. However, this figure is now increasing as digital technology enables more and more people around the world to enjoy its benefits.

Francis Frith's archive is now housed in an historic timber barn in the beautiful village of Teffont in Wiltshire. Its founder would not recognize the archive office as it is today. In place of the many thousands of dusty boxes containing glass plate negatives and an all-pervading odour of photographic chemicals, there are now ranks of computer screens. He would be amazed to watch his images travelling round the world at unimaginable speeds through network and internet lines.

The archive's future is both bright and exciting. Francis Frith, with his unshakeable belief in making photographs available to the greatest number of people, would undoubtedly approve of what is being done today with his lifetime's work. His photographs, depicting our shared past, are now bringing pleasure and enlightenment to millions around the world a century and more after his death.

NOTTINGHAM – *An Introduction*

NOTTINGHAM is a city with a long and turbulent history - the castle, which has been rebuilt several times over the past 1,000 years, is a living symbol of this. From being a walled town, Nottingham expanded dramatically in the nineteenth century, when the Industrial Revolution created new trades; Nottingham's citizens took full advantage of these. Nottingham is now a modern city with a wealth of Victorian buildings and also possessing much of historic interest.

At the dawn of a new millennium, Nottingham can look back with some pride at its history of over 1,000 years. It is said that few events of national importance occurred during Nottingham's history, but throughout the Middle Ages, kings and queens of England made Nottingham Castle their headquarters for the Midlands and the North. Two kings rode out of the castle to fight decisive battles. In 1485, Richard III rode to Bosworth Field where he died in battle; and in 1487, Henry VII rode to East Stoke where he was victorious over the Yorkist army supporting Lambert Simnel. While no major battles were ever fought in Nottingham, during the twelfth and thirteenth centuries the castle was besieged on a number of occasions and the town was sacked and burnt several times.

Charles I chose Nottingham when he made his stand against the Parliamentarians in 1642, although the town's sympathies were divided. The response to his call to arms was only lukewarm, and after staying only a month, he moved on to Shrewsbury.

Nottingham's early history is vague; it was not until 868 that the settlement was mentioned in recorded history, when a Danish army wintered here. In the following decades more Danes settled in the East Midlands, and Nottingham was established as one of the five boroughs of the Danelaw, together with Leicester, Derby, Lincoln and Stamford. The Danish borough was situated on the low plateau where St Mary's church now stands, and the proximity to the River Trent made it strategically important. The first bridge to be built over the river was completed around 920, and the town was then on the direct route from London to York.

The borough then encompassed only a small area surrounding pre-Conquest St

Mary's church - the site of the western rampart can still be seen between Fletcher Gate and Bridlesmith Gate. When William the Conqueror marched northwards with his army in 1068, he chose the hill to the west of the town for his castle. The first buildings were of wood and defences were of earth, but by the end of the twelfth century they were being replaced by stone.

This was the beginning of Nottingham's great involvement in national affairs, although its citizens were probably only aware of this when the town was being attacked. The

Lane and Hurts Yard remain their original width. The wall which encompassed the town was built in the thirteenth and fourteenth centuries, and the borough of Nottingham remained within this until the nineteenth century. The majority of the citizens of Nottingham probably never travelled far beyond the town boundary, but the alabaster ornaments for which the town was famous were sold throughout Europe.

Other trades for which Nottingham was well-known included tanning, brewing, weaving and pottery-making, and several

French borough was situated to the east of the castle with streets leading to the large open area halfway to the English borough, which gradually became the main market place of the town. The medieval town of Nottingham was small, with a population of under 3,000 - Norwich's population at this time was 15,000. Most of the houses and buildings were made of wood, and due to a succession of fires virtually none of them has survived. The layout of the town has remained unchanged to a large extent since then; many streets have been widened, but St James's Street, Bottle

other occupations are still perpetuated by street names such as Pilcher Gate, named for the makers of 'pilchers or furs, and Fletcher Gate, the street of 'fleshers' or butchers.

In the late Middle Ages, the town still had a rural aspect, with many orchards and gardens. The streets, however, were no cleaner than in any other town of the country, and diseases such as the Black Death spread rapidly.

England enjoyed a period of relative peace and prosperity during Tudor times; Nottingham Castle was by this time crumbling away with disuse and became uninhabitable. When the Civil War began in 1642, the castle was repaired by Colonel Hutchinson and held by the Parliamentarians throughout the war, although the town suffered from attacks by Royalist troops. After the war, the remains of the castle were demolished to prevent its further use. The Duke of Newcastle bought the site and began the construction of the present Renaissance building.

Seventeenth and eighteenth century Nottingham was an elegant town; travellers who visited it during that period all commented favourably on the style of the houses and buildings, and on the colonnaded walkway on Long Row. For the wealthy, the town offered a life of pleasurable social rounds, but for the majority of the citizens, life was very difficult and riots were becoming more frequent.

In 1740, the population of Nottingham was still less than 10,000, but overcrowding was becoming a problem. By the end of the century, the population had risen to 29,000. The growth of framework-knitting in the eighteenth century and the apparent prosperity of the town encouraged country people to move into Nottingham. Its boundary was inflexible, however, as the borough freemen would not allow expansion onto the common land north of the borough, nor onto the meadows towards the River Trent. This was the period when the notorious back-to-back houses were built in the remaining open spaces of the borough and on the land evacuated by the wealthy who moved out of the town centre.

At the beginning of the nineteenth century, Nottingham was the centre of the knitwear industry, but the local stocking-knitters were beginning to suffer from a drop in demand for their products, along with price-cutting by the middlemen who controlled the industry. Between 1811 and 1816, there were violent disturbances by the frameworkers in the area - these frameworkers became known as Luddites. Local engineers were then producing machines for the manufacture of lace, which until then had also been a cottage industry. Small factories were opened in the suburbs of Radford and Basford, but it was not until the middle of the nineteenth century that large factories and warehouses were built in Nottingham and the surrounding area.

In 1831, Nottingham suffered from more rioting when mobs, protesting at the rejection of the Reform Bill to extend voting rights, rampaged through the town. After attempting to fire Colwick Hall, they marched up to the castle and set fire to the building, which was gutted. The castle was to remain empty until 1878, when it was opened as a Museum of Art and Science.

Nottingham was finally able to expand beyond its old boundaries in 1845 when the Enclosure Act was passed in Parliament. This allowed building on the town's common lands, although construction was slow to go ahead. Nottingham as a major town may be said to date from 1877 when the suburbs of Sneinton, Basford, Bulwell, Lenton, Radford and Sherwood were incorporated within the borough. The population was then increased from 86,620 to 157,000.

The first major clearance scheme of slum properties in the centre of Nottingham was the destruction in the 1880s of the many yards, known as the Rookeries, that lay between Long Row and Parliament Street.

This allowed the building of King Street and Queen Street, giving easier access into the Great Market Place from the north.

In the 1890s the whole area east of Milton Street was cleared of its warren of houses, and the Victoria Railway Station was then built on the site. The station, which remained for fewer than 70 years, is still remembered with affection by many Nottingham people.

The borough was given city status by Queen Victoria in 1897; the date coincided with her Diamond Jubilee and thus gave the populace a double reason for celebration. The population of the new city was then 239,000 - a figure which has only increased modestly since then. The next period of change in the city was in the 1920s, when Friar Lane was widened, with the consequent loss of Dorothy Vernon's house, which caused a great protest.

The Corporation then proposed the demolition of the Exchange building and the many shops and public houses behind it. This scheme produced an even greater outcry, not only at the cost of building a new town hall but at the realisation that the annual Goose Fair was to be removed from the Market Place. However, this enterprising scheme was approved, and the new Council House has become a source of civic pride.

The house clearance schemes were halted by World War I, but resumed immediately afterwards. A start was made on the back-to-back houses of the Broad Marsh area, which had been a blot on the city's reputation, but this land was to remain largely undeveloped until the 1970's. The year 1928 saw the opening of the new University College at Highfields - the land and money was donated by Sir Jesse Boot - which led in 1948 to the creation of the University of Nottingham. World War II affected the citizens of Nottingham to a much greater degree than World War I. Conscription, evacuation, rationing and air raids became a way of life, but the spirit in which these adversities were overcome was of great value in the postwar years.

The building of new council houses continued after the war: 15,000 were built

between 1945 and 1965. The last two major housing estates to be built were Bestwood and Clifton - the latter being the biggest in the country at the time.

The Victoria Railway Station was closed in 1967 under the Beeching axe; this land and Broad Marsh were then used to build two new-style shopping centres, which were then being planned in Britain. Both these developments, while popular with many people, have not enhanced the skyline of Nottingham and there are now plans in hand to change and enlarge the Broad Marsh Centre.

The next major development in the city was the building of the Royal Centre, which ended a saga extending over 30 years. The complex included a 2,500-seat concert hall and a newly restored Theatre Royal, which had been in danger of closure.

More recently, the old disused land of the Midland Railway and Boots Island Street site have begun to be redeveloped. Following the building of the Inland Revenue complex and Magistrates Courts near Wilford Road, the remainder of the area has been modernised and landscaped. Further east on the Boots site, warehouses which were historically valuable have unfortunately been pulled down, and new buildings are being erected with no apparent consideration to the overall effect.

Fortunately, the Lower Parliament Street area is being revived, with the Sneinton Wholesale Market now converted into retail outlets and the Ice Stadium being replaced by the National Ice Centre. The latter project is important to Nottingham as a whole and to the eastern part of the city in particular, as this has been largely ignored by previous planners.

These photographs are memories of the buildings and streets of Nottingham in a period of its history when it changed more dramatically than in any other century.

The Great Market Place

FOR MANY centuries the trade of the town was centred in the Great Market Place, the largest of its kind in the country. The first market in Nottingham was not held on this site, however, but in the small square known as Weekday Cross where, before the Normans came, a Saxon town had developed on top of the cliff overlooking the Trent valley. After the Normans built their castle on the great rock half a mile to the west, a separate town grew in its shadow and for many years the two communities kept apart. A market to serve the Norman borough sprang up in the open space now known as the Old Market Square, and as the two towns merged the Saxon market place gave way to the larger and more central trading area.

Although the Great Market Place had become the centre of Nottingham's business activities, it was not until 1724 that it acquired a municipal building. Marmaduke Pennel, who was mayor for the year 1724-1725, designed the Exchange, which was built at a cost of £2,400. Among the many rooms used for public purposes was a very large one referred to as the ballroom. Underneath the Exchange and facing the Market Place were four shops, whilst most of the ground floor was taken up by the butchers' stalls, known as the Shambles.

Goose Fair, which for centuries was held in the Market Place, may have originally been held in Weekday Cross. It is a matter of conjecture how old the fair is, but tradition states that it dates from 1284, the year of the charter of Edward I. As with many fairs, Nottingham's fair took place after harvest time, when geese had been fattened on the corn stubble. One of the last deeds of the Mayor of Nottingham was to entertain the burgesses to a feast at which roast goose was the prime joint, and this custom was observed until 1781.

The fair was originally intended as a mart, but during the last century it has become a pleasure fair. The last fair to be held in the square was in 1927, when the crowds saw a new feature on the skyline - the framework of the new Council House. With the construction of the Processional Way and the flowerbeds, the covered market was removed from its age-old site. Roundabouts and stalls are occasionally brought back to the Market Place, but the old atmosphere can never return.

THE MARKET PLACE
1890 22808

THE MARKET PLACE 1890 22807

On market day the whole square was full of activity and people came into Nottingham from all the surrounding villages. In the foreground, in the area known as the Stones, is the pot market where goods were spread out among the straw.

MARKET STREET 1890 22812

On the left is the Talbot, which was opened in 1874 as a drinking palace - it was filled with sculptures and bronzes. In 1929, Yates Wine Lodges bought the Talbot and it still remains a great attraction.

THE MARKET PLACE 1890 22809

In this view of the market place, the Exchange can be seen in the background. This building was designed in 1724 by the mayor, Marmaduke Pennel, but was largely rebuilt in 1814. Behind the Exchange was a multitude of commercial buildings, including the butchers' stalls known as the Shambles.

LONG ROW 1890 22815
This was the last decade when horse-drawn traffic reigned supreme on Nottingham's streets. Most of these buildings on Long Row were soon to be rebuilt, including the fine white Georgian House in the centre.

THE MARKET PLACE 1902 48321
Electric trams were now replacing horse trams and rebuilding was taking place on Long Row. In the background is the Exchange; although the largest building in the market place, it was not grand or overpowering.

THE MARKET PLACE 1906 56461
The covered colonnade, which has protected shoppers for generations, is still a feature of Long Row. Samuel's the jewellers and Hepworth's the tailors, on the right, are two of the well-known businesses in the row.

LONG ROW EAST 1902 48326
Crowds are thronging the Market Place and Long
Row giving little heed to the traffic. The Black Boy
Hotel stands splendidly in the centre, with its
astonishing wealth of architectural detail. The flags
were flying to celebrate the end of the Boer War.
The electric trams which began service in 1901
quickly proved popular with the citizens
of Nottingham.

THE STATUE OF QUEEN VICTORIA 1906 56462
The statue had been unveiled the previous year amid general acclamation, but 50 years later the statue, the only one in the city centre, was removed to the Victoria Embankment. In the foreground, a woman is choosing from the pots laid out on the traditional site of the Stones.

THE MARKET PLACE 1923 74594

The statue of Queen Victoria is on the right and beneath it are two of Nottingham's other fixtures - Solari's and Capocci's ice-cream stalls. Griffin & Spalding's Victorian department store in the centre was soon to be demolished and rebuilt.

THE COUNCIL HOUSE c1955 N50046

After the smaller scale Exchange, the new Council House of Portland stone seemed very grandiose to the citizens of Nottingham, but they have come to appreciate their imposing town hall. For some years after being built, it was still referred to as the Exchange and the renamed Old Market Square was dubbed Slab Square.

THE OLD MARKET SQUARE c1950 N50054

A busy and sunny square with vehicles parked on the road in front of the Council House, although the forecourt was for official cars only. Before the two shopping centres were built in Nottingham, the square was a mecca for most shoppers.

THE OLD MARKET SQUARE c1950 N50056

Another moment in the square caught by the camera. This appears to be lunchtime judging by the number of people taking their ease. In the centre background, the traditional building of Lloyds Bank can be seen, and on the extreme left is a branch of Fifty Shilling Tailors.

Around the City

IN 1890, when the earliest photographs in this book were taken, Nottingham had developed from being a compact market town into a borough with a population of approximately 214,000. The scope of these photographs, however, only extends to main streets, public buildings, churches and views - few photographers were exploring the back streets of Victorian towns.

Nottingham was already priding itself on being the 'Queen of the Midlands' and its municipal buildings, parks and leisure facilities were admired both within and beyond the town boundary. The boulevards which had been built in the 1880s were not, however, matched in the centre of the town, which had mainly narrow streets. This was to change in the 1890s, when a great swathe was cut through the slums in the Charlotte Street area in preparation for the construction of the Victoria Railway Station.

When Nottingham was given the status of a city in 1897, one authority described it as 'a large and improving town', but very little further change was to occur for the next 25 years.

Industrially, great changes were taking place in the city. Lace making and hosiery knitting were still the principal trades, but along with these traditional enterprises, three new industries had begun in the last quarter of the nineteenth century. Three men, one from Nottingham and the other two who made their names here, began separately to create a major new industry in the town. Jesse Boot, from humble beginnings as a herbalist, created a manufacturing and retailing business which is still the leading private employer in the city. There had been a small tobacco factory in Nottingham for over 50 years when John Player took it over in 1877, but it was in the late 1890s when the great expansion in the business took place which led in 1901 to the foundation of the Imperial Tobacco Company.

The third great new industry of the town - the Raleigh Cycle Company - was founded by Frank Bowden, who in 1887 invested in a small bicycle works and within a few years had created the world's largest bicycle factory. Without these three major companies, Nottingham would have suffered more severely from the slump in trade in the 1920s and 1930s and the decline in the lace industry.

The inter-war years saw the almost complete clearance of the condemned houses in the Broad Marsh area, which had blighted Nottingham's reputation for so long. Civic pride was enhanced with the demolition of the old Exchange and its replacement by the Council House, while the building of the University College at Highfields was equally significant culturally. When World War II began in 1939, Nottingham was poised to continue the changes and modernisation of the city, but this was to be delayed for another 20 years - with important consequences.

LONG ROW EAST 1890 22814
Many well-known businesses had their premises in this area, including Skinner & Rook, Dixon & Parker and Joseph Burton. The building on the right at the bottom of Pelham Street was soon to be demolished and replaced by Boots the Chemists.

VICTORIA STREET 1890 22817

The lower buildings on the right were demolished during the building of the Great Central Railway in the late 1890s. The Nottingham Joint Stock Bank, later the Midland Bank, who had premises further up the street, then bought the plot of land adjoining its old building and built an imposing new office.

CARRINGTON STREET 1890 22819

The street was then lined with houses, small shops and public houses. There is a policeman performing traffic duty at the junction with Canal Street, but the traffic - all horse-drawn - is very light.

CHEAPSIDE 1890 22821
This street derived its name from the Old English word 'cepe', meaning bargain. The building to the right of Beecroft's was the Tudor house of the Earl of Mansfield. All these buildings were pulled down to make way for the new Council House in the 1920s.

CHEAPSIDE 1890 22822

A busy scene looking towards the Market Place. The pavement on the right was the pitch for women flower-sellers on Wednesdays and Saturdays, creating a splash of colour. Beecroft's, on the right, was an old-established toy and fancy-goods shop.

PELHAM STREET 1900 22823

On the right is Boots the Chemist's first shop in Pelham Street, opened in 1892. This was Jesse Boot's finest shop to date. When, in 1903, the Corporation cleared High Street of all its old properties, he seized the opportunity to build an even more splendid shop here.

ST PETER'S CHURCH 1890 22834
St Peter's Square was the terminus of the horse tramway routes to Trent Bridge and West Bridgford. Wheeler Gate in the foreground was in the process of being widened, and Swann's provision stores had recently been demolished.

ST MARY'S CHURCH 1890 22827

ST MARY'S CHURCH 1890

The Mother Church of Nottingham has the appearance, if not the stature, of a cathedral. Mentioned in the Domesday Book, the present building dates from the fifteenth century. The church was in danger of collapsing in the nineteenth century and was completely restored by Sir Gilbert Scott and William Moffatt.

THE COUNTY LUNATIC ASYLUM
Ransom Road 1890

This was built in 1857-59 by T C Hine and was also known as Dr Tate's Asylum after the medical superintendent who served here for the first 54 years of its existence. This asylum later became the Coppice Hospital.

THE COUNTY LUNATIC ASYLUM, RANSOM ROAD 1890 22851

THE ARBORETUM 1890
The original idea behind the creation of the Arboretum was to give the citizens of Nottingham a scenic park in which to relax. However, for the first few years after its opening in 1852 the public were admitted free of charge on only three days a week, while there was an admission charge of 6d for adults and 3d for children on other days.

THE ARBORETUM 1890 24714

THE ARBORETUM 1902 48331

THE POOR LAW OFFICES, SHAKESPEARE STREET 1890 24710

These were built in 1887 at a cost of £14,000. In the blitz on Nottingham in May 1941, the building, then occupied by the Registrar of Births, Marriages and Deaths, was completely gutted; it was subsequently rebuilt.

ST BARNABAS' CATHEDRAL 1890 22839

The cathedral was built on land then outside the town in 1841-44. The cost of the building and the land was £20,000, and its construction was very controversial - it was described as the new Romish Meeting House on Derby Road.

THE FOREST RACECOURSE 1893 33255
On the left is the grandstand designed by John Carr and built in 1777. In the front was a platform for viewing and there was room for 500 people on the roof. The last meeting on the Forest took place on 30th September 1890.

KING STREET AND QUEEN STREET 1902 48322
Two grim buildings from the last decade of the nineteenth century. The building on the left was the General Post Office from 1898 to 1972, and the building in the centre was designed by Alfred Waterhouse for the Prudential Assurance Company.

WHEELER GATE 1902 48327

Until 1885, Wheeler Gate was a narrow street only wide enough for one vehicle to pass at a time. The western side was then demolished and rebuilt, but it was another seven years before the eastern side was pulled down to give the road the width which exists today.

VICTORIA RAILWAY STATION 1902 48325
The station was opened in May 1900 without ceremony - and closed 67 years later with as little ceremony. The clock tower, which is the only part of the station to survive, stands as a sad memento of this great building.

THEATRE SQUARE 1920 69429

Two of these buildings have now disappeared, as has the statue in the foreground. The Hippodrome Cinema, later the Gaumont, remained open until 1971, and the County Hotel, next to the Theatre Royal, closed in 1976. The statue of Samuel Morley was removed in 1927 and was unfortunately smashed in transit.

THE FLYING HORSE HOTEL 1920 69427

The hotel was one of the landmarks of Nottingham for centuries and it is a matter of conjecture how it came by its unusual name. The original building was Tudor, but it has a history of rebuilding.

THEATRE SQUARE 1927 80549

An almost deserted Theatre Square, laid with granite setts. The Theatre Royal on the left was built in 1865 by William and John Lambert, and designed to dominate the view up Market Street. In 1969, when the theatre was in danger of closure, the Corporation stepped in and bought it, and it was then incorporated into the Royal Centre.

THEATRE SQUARE 1927 80550

Two splendid motor cars are in front of the Theatre Royal, but a horse-drawn vehicle is also in view. The site of Samuel Morley's statue is now replaced by a traffic island, near which is a policeman on point duty, with only jay-walkers requiring his control.

THE LAKE AND PAVILION, HIGHFIELDS 1928 81571
The University Park was laid out in 1924 and was immediately a great attraction to Nottingham people. Highfields Lido was opened in the same year and continued in use until 1981.

UNIVERSITY COLLEGE 1928 81572

This was the year in which the college was opened by King George V. Sir Jesse Boot, who donated the land and financed the building of the college, was unable to attend the opening ceremony owing to his disabilities, but afterwards the King and Queen took tea with him.

WOLLATON HALL 1928 81579
The hall was owned by Lord Middleton until 1924, when he sold it to the Corporation of Nottingham for £200,000. The city immediately recouped this sum by selling part of the estate for house building. Wollaton Hall, which is one of the most important sixteenth century buildings in the country, now contains a natural history museum; the house and its park are a great amenity to the city.

WOLLATON HALL c1955 N50022

WOLLATON HALL 1928 81579

Nottingham Castle

VIEWED against the background of history, the present building on the castle rock is quite modern, but the whole history of Nottingham has revolved around this prominence.

It has been the centre of much activity since William the Conqueror recognised the rock as the best defensive point in the area, and commanded William Peverel to build a castle on it. Since then the castle has been the home of kings, queens and princes. It has seen the crusading Richard the Lionheart, the infamous King John, and Charles Stuart raising his standard to call his supporters to his side at the outbreak of the Civil War.

It was here that the young Edward III trapped his mother Queen Isabella and her lover Roger Mortimer, and created one of the castle's most popular and enduring legends - the story of Mortimer's hole.

During the brief reign of Richard III, the castle was the king's principal residence, and thereafter the great tower which he had completed was known as Richard's Tower. In August 1485, when Richard learnt that Henry Tudor had landed in Wales and marched to Lichfield, he rode with his troops out of his Castle of Care for the last time.

With the fall of Richard, the glory of the castle as a stronghold had gone. Richard's successor Henry VII felt that the numerous strong castles held by nobles were a menace to his rule and allowed them to fall into disrepair. In 1487, however, Henry made the castle the headquarters from which his army marched to East Stoke to repel the supporters of Lambert Simnel, the pretender to the throne.

Nottingham Castle, if we believe the legends, was where Robin Hood and his followers carried out their most impudent sallies against the Sheriff of Nottingham. We may have to admit to inconsistencies in the stories and facts relating to Robin Hood, but he has now become the most well-known Nottingham figure of all.

Nearer our own times, the angry Reform Act rioters swarmed to the rock and set fire to the castle. Fortunately, the castle was empty at the time and was no longer an impregnable fortress but an Italianate palace. The owner, the Duke of Newcastle, was awarded £21,000 as compensation for the destruction of the building; but he allowed it to remain in a ruinous state for over 45 years before leasing it to the Corporation of Nottingham.

For the last century, apart from World War II when it was requisitioned by the military, the castle and its grounds have been an oasis for the citizens of Nottingham and its visitors.

THE CASTLE FROM THE PARK 1893 33239
Looking rather out of place on a hill-top in a Midlands city, the Renaissance palace is a great disappointment to those visitors who expect to see a Norman castle.

THE CASTLE GATEHOUSE 1890 22843
The gatehouse or outer barbican is the last surviving
remains of the medieval castle. Built in the thirteenth
century, it was in a ruinous state in 1908 when the
Corporation began its restoration, which unfortunately
took away most of its character.

THE CASTLE GATEHOUSE 1920 69431

In this view of the reconstructed gatehouse, remnants of the original medieval stonework can still be seen - a reminder of the old Norman castle.

NOTTINGHAM CASTLE 1890 22845

This view of the castle was taken from the site of the medieval pond, which supplied fresh fish to the inhabitants of the castle. Following a collapse of the rock face in 1996, access to the terrace overlooking the Meadows has been restricted until repairs have been completed.

PARK STEPS 1920 69433
This was an ancient path between Lenton and Nottingham. The steps were cut when the Duke of Newcastle began to develop the Park Estate in 1829. They lead from Park Valley to the Ropewalk.

THE CASTLE
From Nottingham Canal 1893 33240
This was the time when most of the country's
heavy goods were still transported by barge.
Below the castle, a new tree-lined boulevard was
built in 1884.

THE CASTLE GATEHOUSE 1920 69434
The well laid out flowerbeds and lawns are an attraction to both Nottingham residents and visitors. The view towards the city has now unfortunately been spoilt by tall office blocks and multi-storey carparks.

NOTTINGHAM GENERAL HOSPITAL 1920 69436

The hospital was founded in 1783, and the original building is still part of the present structure. Following the closure of the hospital in 1992, the main building and the Round Tower of the Jubilee Wing were taken over by Nottingham Health Authority. This view of the hospital was taken from the Castle green.

NURSE'S HOME, LENTON ROAD 1923 74597

The picture was taken in the year in which the home was opened by the Prince of Wales. The house was built as a war memorial for the city and county, and provided 130 rooms. Following the closure of the hospital, the building is being converted into luxury apartments.

STATUE OF ALBERT BALL 1923 74598
Captain Albert Ball, VC was the great flying ace of World War I; he was killed in action at the age of 20. It was suggested that the statue should be sculpted by Auguste Rodin, but he declined, and the work was executed by Henry Poole.

THE ZIG-ZAG WALK 1923 74601

This was a popular walk to the summit of Nottingham Castle rock, but it is now in a dangerous and overgrown condition.

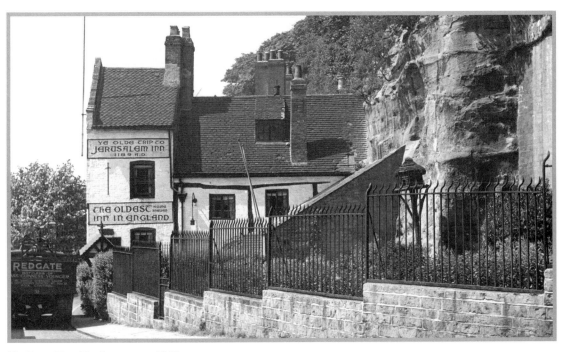

YE OLDE TRIP TO JERUSALEM 1949 N50041

The age of this inn is conjectural, but its fame has spread throughout the country. Several rooms have been hewn out of the sandstone rock and beneath the inn are deep cellars and caves.

STATUE OF ROBIN HOOD C1955 N50090
For hundreds of years, the names of Robin Hood and Nottingham have been inseparably linked, yet it was not until 1952, through the generosity of Nottingham businessman Philip Clay, that the city acquired a statue of its most famous character. It is positioned just outside the castle walls.

The River Trent

THE FIRST settlers of Nottingham were the Anglo-Saxons who occupied the area where St Mary's church now stands from around the sixth century, no doubt influenced by the proximity of the River Trent. The Danes, who raided the settlement and took possession of it in the ninth century, were the first people to take full advantage of the river's potential as a means of transportation.

The first bridge over the Trent was built around 920 by Edward the Elder. This had stone piers on oak piles and was replaced in 1156 by a second bridge known as the Hethbethebrigg - there is no definitive spelling of the name and the meaning of this word is unknown.

Like most bridges of its time, Trent Bridge had its own chapel; in 1303 a charity was formed to provide two chaplains to celebrate divine service daily 'for the souls of all Christians who assigned goods to the maintenance of the bridge'.

During the Middle Ages, the bridge was in constant need of repair, but in 1335 and 1684 the bridge had to be completely rebuilt after severe damage by ice. Two arches, which are still to be seen in the middle of the traffic island at the southern end of Trent Bridge, are all that remain of the fourteenth century bridge.

By the nineteenth century, the medieval bridge was outdated and was discovered to be in danger of collapsing. Between 1867-71, a new bridge was built a few yards downstream of the old one.

In 1895, a great frost which lasted for several weeks caused the river to freeze over completely. Fires were lit on the ice and skating was enjoyed by many local people.

Spring floods were an annual occurrence in the meadows bordering the river and a wooden causeway, known as the Cheyney Bridges, was built over the marshland in the eighteenth century. Paintings of the town show the land between the river and the town to be covered by a carpet of blue crocuses.

Towards the end of the nineteenth century, the citizens of Nottingham were able to take advantage of the increasing leisure activities available on or near the river. Excursions to Wilford and Clifton had long been popular, but pleasure steamers were introduced on the river and a promenade was constructed along the riverbank from Wilford Bridge to Trent Bridge.

Nottingham's proximity to a navigable river that was also fordable has played a great part in the city's success. By the twentieth century, Nottingham was a major inland port with huge petrol tankers plying from Hull to Colwick. Since the decrease in the transport of goods by water, the growth in the leisure boat industry has given the river a new lease of life.

TRENT BRIDGE 1902 48329

LANDING STAGES, TURNEY'S QUAY 1893 33248
In the background is the iron-girder bridge of the Midland Railway which was converted into a road bridge in 1979.

TRENT BRIDGE 1890 24720
The bridge that was built in 1871 replaced the medieval bridge, which was in danger of collapsing. For a while, the old and the new bridges stood side by side, and for long after, Nottingham folk would talk of going down to the bridges.

TRENT BRIDGE CRICKET GROUND 1893
The ground was established in 1838 by William Clarke, and for the next 20 years he promoted a series of cricket matches which led to the formation of the Nottingham Cricket Club. The pavilion was built in 1886 and was not altered significantly for the next 100 years.

◆

TRENT BRIDGE CRICKET GROUND 1893 33250

TRENT BRIDGE CRICKET GROUND 1893 33249

TRENT BRIDGE 1902 48328
Here we can see A J Witty's pleasure steamers 'Sunbeam'
and 'Queen' at Turney's Quay. River trips were becoming
so popular that a third vessel was required, the 'Empress',
which was also built at Witty's boatyard. This boat was
sunk in 1940 while on its second crossing to Dunkirk
during the evacuation from France.

RIVER TRENT BENEATH CLIFTON GROVE 1893 33253

For many years this was the area where Nottingham folk would stroll or row. After taking a tram or trolley-bus ride to Wilford Bridge, a walk to Clifton would perhaps be followed by tea at a cottage on the Green.

VICTORIA EMBANKMENT STEPS 1920 69443

The citizens of Nottingham are fortunate in having a stretch of river in the city that is relatively unspoilt by industry.

TRENT BRIDGE FROM LOVERS' WALK 1927 80552

By 1924, the increase in traffic necessitated the widening of the bridge and this was undertaken at a cost of £130,000. During World War II, a temporary Bailey Bridge was stored for use in the event of Trent Bridge being bombed.

THE ARCH OF REMEMBRANCE, VICTORIA EMBANKMENT GARDENS 1928 81563
These gardens were laid out in 1927 on land donated by Sir Jesse Boot, who had originally planned this site for the new University College. The War Memorial was designed by T Wallis Gordon and unveiled in November 1927.

RIVER TRENT c1955 N50079
One of the favourite venues for Nottingham people - the embankment steps on a warm summer's day attracting families and swans. The boat trips down the river to Colwick and occasionally to Radcliffe-on-Trent have always been popular.

RIVER TRENT c1955 N50082
The riverbank on a summer's day, people out for a stroll, children frolicking and folk sitting on the grass - the scene never changes.

**VICTORIA EMBANKMENT
MEMORIAL GARDENS c1955**
The statue of Queen Victoria is gazing over the ornamental gardens by the River Trent. The statue had stood in the Old Market Square for 48 years until it was removed in 1953 and replaced by a traffic island.

◆

VICTORIA EMBANKMENT c1955
The embankment borders a curve of the river and is a mile-and-a-quarter long. Nottingham folk have been coming here to relax and stroll under the trees for over a century.

VICTORIA EMBANKMENT MEMORIAL GARDENS c1955 N50085

VICTORIA EMBANKMENT c1955 N50081

**THE SUSPENSION BRIDGE, RIVER TRENT
c1955**
This elegant bridge was built in 1906
primarily to carry water pipes from
Wilford Hill Reservoir to the Meadows
and also as a footbridge over the River
Trent.

VICTORIA EMBANKMENT AND TRENT BRIDGE c1955 N50083

THE SUSPENSION BRIDGE, RIVER TRENT c1955 N50303

THE SUSPENSION BRIDGE, RIVER TRENT c1955 N50302
The design of the two arches carrying the cables was matched in the 1920s when the Memorial Arch to the dead of World War I was built nearby.

The City in the 1950s

THE 1950s was the decade which saw the beginning of a change in Nottingham and in the lifestyle of its inhabitants. During World War II and the years of austerity afterwards, the civic authorities, while planning for the future, did not fulfil their promises. In 1943, a civic centre was planned to be built between Burton Street and Forest Road, but this scheme never came to fruition. Priority was given to house-building; but progress was slow, and as a short-term expedient 2,000 prefabricated houses were purchased for use in Beechdale and Aspley.

The quincentenary in 1949 of the granting of the Great Charter to Nottingham by Henry VI, and the Festival of Britain two years later, were opportunities for the citizens of Nottingham to visit exhibitions around the city. Both these events were stimulating, and were a great boost to morale following the deprivations of the previous years.

The Coronation of Queen Elizabeth II in 1953 and the huge increase in television viewing that it provoked displaced cinema-going as the foremost leisure activity. Live theatre was still very popular, however. The Playhouse in Goldsmith Street, although run on a shoestring, was producing a consistently high level of entertainment. Members of the repertory company then included Derek Godfrey, Graham Crowden, Michael Barrington, Daphne Slater and Joan Plowright. It was not until 1963, after great controversy, that the new Playhouse in East Circus Street was opened.

The Theatre Royal was at the same time showing a variety of plays, pantomimes, ballets and operas. Great actors such as John Gielgud, Laurence Olivier and Donald Wolfit could be seen here; at 15 years of age, Julie Andrews appeared in the 1950-51 pantomime; and during the summer months, Harry Hanson's Court Players would play repertory. In 1952 Agatha Christie's play 'The Mousetrap' and in 1953 her 'Witness for the Prosecution' were given their premieres at the Theatre Royal.

The Empire Theatre was in its last decade of existence, but was still giving twice-nightly shows with the great comedians of the day, including Laurel and Hardy at Christmas 1953. After its closure in 1958, the site was to remain undeveloped for another 20 years until the long awaited concert hall was built.

During the 1950s, the authorities were struggling with the problem of the huge increase in traffic on Nottingham's roads. Their original plan was to build an urban motorway around the city centre and a rapid transit rail system. Work commenced on a dual-carriageway road from Canal Street to Friar Lane in the late 1950s, but the controversy caused by the consequent demolition of many historic buildings brought about the abandonment of the planned road beyond Chapel Bar.

Nottingham's road problems were not solved by this cancellation, but the planners were forced to consider public opinion more fully in their future deliberations.

LONG ROW EAST c1955 N50053
The Long Row frontage is dominated by the Black Boy
Hotel with its fantastically decorated façade. This
famous Watson Fothergill building was to remain for
only a further 14 years before being replaced by a
faceless shop. This was obviously a time when cars were
allowed to park without restriction.

THE FLYING HORSE HOTEL c1955 N50092

The hotel was renovated in 1936 and the façade was redesigned with plasterwork copied from the Rose & Crown at Saffron Walden. In 1967 it was proposed to demolish the inn, but the application was refused. However, in 1987 it was converted into a shopping arcade.

DERBY ROAD c1955 N50063

The Three Horse Shoes public house on the left and the Albert Hotel on the right have been pulled down. The stonework of St Barnabas' cathedral has been cleaned and the interior has also been restored.

CHEAPSIDE C1955 N50057
This is one of the streets in Nottingham that has a different name for each side. Long queues for buses were commonplace then, as buses were still the primary means of transport for most citizens.

ANGEL ROW AND LONG ROW WEST 1949 N50061
On the right, Pearson Bros, Farmer's music store, TN Parr's pork shop and the Cavendish furniture store were well-established businesses. The film being shown at the Odeon cinema on the left was 'The Bad Lord Byron', starring Dennis Price and Joan Greenwood.

MARKET STREET c1955 N50050
Here, the Theatre Royal is closing the vista to the north. Until 1864, this was a narrow alley called Sheep Lane, but after demolishing many old properties this street was created. Originally renamed Theatre Street, the populace took exception to this name and it was then changed to Market Street.

CLUMBER STREET c1955 N50301
Although it was a one-way street for traffic, in this photograph Clumber Street has the appearance of being a precinct, with shoppers walking in the road. In the background is the Milton's Head Hotel, a Victorian public house which seemed to be a fixture until the construction of the Victoria Shopping Centre.

QUEEN STREET c1955 N50052

A view of two late-Victorian buildings facing each other across Queen Street. The General Post Office on the left opened in 1898 and was used as such until 1972, when the Post Office moved to a new building higher up the street. Alfred Waterhouse's Prudential building on the right was built in the style of its London head office.

LOWER PARLIAMENT STREET c1955 N50060

A mixture of architectural styles are on the left, including two old houses, the entrance archway to the old St Stephen's church and the south entrance to the Victoria Railway Station. All these structures were demolished when the Victoria Shopping Centre was built in the early 1970s.

THEATRE SQUARE 1949 N50066
Donald Wolfit and his wife Rosalind Iden were appearing at the
Theatre Royal in a series of Shakespearean plays. As a teenager
Donald Wolfit was already stage-struck; he would cycle from
Newark to attend matinées here, little dreaming that he would
one day be performing on its stage.

UPPER PARLIAMENT STREET c1955 N50064
The nearest tall building on the left is the Skin Clinic, originally the Turkish Baths, and beyond it is the News Theatre. This was opened in 1914 as the Regal Cinema and converted into the News Theatre in 1935. In 1956, it was renamed the Odd Hour Cinema before closing in 1957.

CHAPEL BAR c1955 N50062
This was the site of the ancient gateway into Nottingham from the west until 1743. The building on the left is Hickling's Vaults, which was demolished in 1961, revealing several caves and part of the old town wall underneath.

BRIDLESMITH GATE c1955 N50058

This street, which was once the main road into Nottingham from the south and crowded with people and traffic, is now pedestrianised and the direct route between the city's two shopping centres. On the left at the corner of Pepper Street is Lloyd's Coffee House, famous for its cakes and pastries.

KING STREET c1955 N50051
This is the street which, along with Queen Street, was cut through the infamous Rookeries in the 1880s. The Rookeries were the alleyways packed with slum dwellings which were giving Nottingham such a bad reputation for housing. Jessop's department store on the right is another of Watson Fothergill's richly decorated buildings.

Index

Acknowledgement

The City of Nottingham: Local Studies Library for the loan of some of these photographs.

To receive your FREE Mounted Print

Cut out this Voucher and return it with your remittance for £1.50 to cover postage and handling. Choose any photograph included in this book. Your SEPIA print will be A4 in size, and mounted in a cream mount with burgundy rule lines, overall size 14 x 11 inches.

Order additional Mounted Prints at HALF PRICE (only £7.49 each*)

If there are further pictures you would like to order, possibly as gifts for friends and family, acquire them at half price (no additional postage and handling required).

Have your Mounted Prints framed*

For an additional £14.95 per print you can have your chosen Mounted Print framed in an elegant polished wood and gilt moulding, overall size 16 x 13 inches (no additional postage and handling required).

---

* IMPORTANT!
These special prices are only available if ordered using the original voucher on this page (no copies permitted) and at the same time as your free Mounted Print, for delivery to the same address

---

Voucher for FREE and Reduced Price Frith Prints

Picture no.	Page number	Qty	Mounted @ £7.49	Framed + £14.95	Total Cost
		1	**Free of charge***	£	£
			£	£	£
			£	£	£
			£	£	£
			£	£	£
			£	£	£

* Post & handling	£1.50
Total Order Cost	£

Title: AROUND NOTTINGHAM
060-8

Please do not photocopy this voucher. Only the original is valid, so please cut it out and return it to us.

I enclose a cheque / postal order for £ . . . .
made payable to 'The Francis Frith Collection'
OR please debit my Mastercard / Visa / Switch / Amex card

Number . . . .

Expires . . . . Signature . . . .

Name Mr/Mrs/Ms . . . .

Address . . . .

. . . .

. . . .

. . . . Postcode . . . .

Daytime Tel No . . . .   Valid to 31/12/01

Frith Collectors' Guild

From time to time we publish a magazine of news and stories about Frith photographs and further special offers of Frith products. If you would like 12 months FREE membership, please return this form and we will send you a New Member Pack.

Send completed forms to:
The Francis Frith Collection, Frith's Barn, Teffont, Salisbury, Wiltshire SP3 5QP

The Francis Frith Collectors' Guild

I would like to receive the New Members Pack offering 12 months FREE membership.
060-8

Name Mr/Mrs/Ms . . . .
Address . . . .
. . . .
. . . .
. . . . Postcode . . . .

Frith Book Co 1999 Titles

From 2000 we aim at publishing 100 new books each year. For latest catalogue please contact Frith Book Co

Barnstaple	1-85937-084-5	£12.99	Oct 99		Maidstone	1-85937-056-X	£12.99	Sep 99
Blackpool	1-85937-049-7	£12.99	Sep 99		Northumberland	1-85937-072-1		
Bognor Regis	1-85937-055-1	£12.99	Sep 99		& Tyne and Wear		£14.99	Sep 99
Bristol	1-85937-050-0	£12.99	Sep 99		North Yorkshire	1-85937-048-9	£14.99	Sep 99
Cambridge	1-85937-092-6	£12.99	Oct 99		Nottingham	1-85937-060-8	£12.99	Sep 99
Cambridgeshire	1-85937-086-1	£14.99	Nov 99		Oxfordshire	1-85937-076-4	£14.99	Oct 99
Cheshire	1-85937-045-4	£14.99	Sep 99		Penzance	1-85937-069-1	£12.99	Sep 99
Chester	1-85937-090-X	£12.99	Nov 99		Reading	1-85937-087-X	£12.99	Nov 99
Chesterfield	1-85937-071-3	£12.99	Sep 99		St Ives	1-85937-068-3	£12.99	Sep 99
Chichester	1-85937-089-6	£12.99	Nov 99		Salisbury	1-85937-091-8	£12.99	Nov 99
Cornwall	1-85937-054-3	£14.99	Sep 99		Scarborough	1-85937-104-3	£12.99	Sep 99
Cotswolds	1-85937-099-3	£14.99	Nov 99		Scottish Castles	1-85937-077-2	£14.99	Oct 99
					Sevenoaks	1-85937-057-8		
					and Tonbridge		£12.99	Sep 99
					Sheffield	1-85937-070-5		
					and S Yorkshire		£12.99	Sep 99
					Shropshire	1-85937-083-7	£14.99	Nov 99
					Southampton	1-85937-088-8	£12.99	Nov 99
					Staffordshire	1-85937-047-0	£14.99	Sep 99
					Stratford	1-85937-098-5		
					upon Avon		£12.99	Nov 99
					Suffolk	1-85937-074-8	£14.99	Oct 99
					Surrey	1-85937-081-0	£14.99	Oct 99
					Torbay	1-85937-063-2	£12.99	Sep 99
					Wiltshire	1-85937-053-5	£14.99	Sep 99

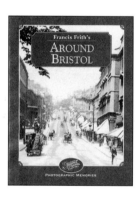
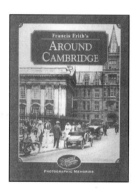

Derby	1-85937-046-2	£12.99	Sep 99
Devon	1-85937-052-7	£14.99	Sep 99
Dorset	1-85937-075-6	£14.99	Oct 99
Dorset Coast	1-85937-062-4	£14.99	Sep 99
Dublin	1-85937-058-6	£12.99	Sep 99
East Anglia	1-85937-059-4	£14.99	Sep 99
Eastbourne	1-85937-061-6	£12.99	Sep 99
English Castles	1-85937-078-0	£14.99	Oct 99
Essex	1-85937-082-9	£14.99	Nov 99
Falmouth	1-85937-066-7	£12.99	Sep 99
Hampshire	1-85937-064-0	£14.99	Sep 99
Hertfordshire	1-85937-079-9	£14.99	Nov 99
Isle of Man	1-85937-065-9	£14.99	Sep 99
Liverpool	1-85937-051-9	£12.99	Sep 99

British Life A Century Ago
246 x 189mm 144pp, hardback. Black and white Lavishly illustrated with photos from the turn of the century, and with extensive commentary. It offers a unique insight into the social history and heritage of bygone Britain.

1-85937-103-5 £17.99 ....

Available from your local bookshop or from the publisher